West of Paradise

West of Paradise

New Poems by

George Venn

ICE
RIVER
PRESS

1999

Other Works by George Venn

Poems
Sunday Afternoon: Grande Ronde (1975)
Off the Main Road (1978)

Essays/Fiction/ Poetry/Translations
Marking the Magic Circle (1987)

Edited Collections
Eastern Oregon Literary Supplement (1971-73)
The Oregon Literature Series, Vols. I-VI., (1989-1994)
River Hills Rounded With Wind (1997)
Pulling Together (1997)
Cascade Crest Trailhead Book (1998)

Copyright for Author © 1999
Ice River Press
an imprint of
Wordcraft of Oregon
P.O. Box 3235
La Grande, OR 97850
wordcraft@oregontrail.net

ISBN: 1-877655-31-7
First Edition
November 1999

Cover photo by permission of David Jensen
Cover design by Brian C. Clark
Special Thanks to those anonymous Oregon literati
whose generous donation helped make this book possible.

Printed in the U.S. by Complete Reproduction Service, Santa Ana, CA

WEST OF PARADISE

George Venn

CONTENTS

I. In Blue Mountains

II. Interior Columbia: In and Out of Towns

III. Segues for Interstate 84

IV. Voice Lessons in Hell's Canyon

V. Into the Pacific

VI. Heart of the Valley

I.

IN BLUE MOUNTAINS

JANUARY: A LETTER

Dear Careless Love–

Here, it is morning. Hoarfrost and fog.
The winter hawk flies low
enough for you to see her
infinite black eyes
and every tree's needles
are redefined
by this crystalline shade–
this argument that
the delicate is huge.

At the mailbox
I fell–ass over teakettle–
where hoarfrost hid the ice
–go ahead and laugh–
and I sat there wondering how
long before the sun would open–
my life at zero
freezing in my throat
when winter hawk suddenly
slid out of the fog again
just overhead. There is
this argument that
the delicate is starving.

I got up, raised the red
flag on the box, put this
letter inside. Already, I
was starting to chatter.
Ice crystals began to form
in my nostrils. My face was gone.
There was no argument now.
An isolate wing called winter was
about to hit me–again–

10

just as I closed the door.

Love, this letter–
I hope this gets through
all this weather to you–
somehow. Please–
write me at the old Star
Route address. Remember?

THE EMPEROR BREEDS ONLY ON THE ICE

after Robert Ardrey

When late February comes, and southern autumn
darkens into winter, pairs of emperor penguins
march inland across the Antarctic ice
to that place where they must breed.

On fathomless freeze, she lays their single egg
and he picks up the egg on his foot.
Then she and her friends go back to the sea–
their only source of food.

Close among the circle of males,
each with an egg on his foot, he remains.
They begin to move. Perpetual night encloses them.
The zero winter blows, shudders,

snaps, crushes, torments them now
as it has tormented every year.
Each stands with an egg on his foot.
Shoulder to shoulder, they preserve their heat.

There are no fights over property,
dominance, borders, ideologies.
Once, twice, the night clears.
They see the Southern Cross–its crucifixion clear.

The southern aurora displays its veils–
faraway, shifting, impalpable,
tantalizing, rewardless.
More often, the storm whites them out.

Wind cuts cold beyond calculation.
For two months on that fathomless ice,
they live the terror of soft illumination
and they revolve there–

this fasting masculine mass–
each with an egg on his foot
presenting this one on the edge to hostility
giving that one at the center a moment of warmth.

Can we apprehend these nights?
In a mass of male emperor penguins?
Revolving? Each with an egg
on his foot?

In a dark, frozen, endless Antarctic?
Beneath withdrawn stars?
You do not know, I shall not know.
We must learn this kind of love.

FIVE SIX MINUTES IN MARCH

Morning, that red cockadoodlum, calls me
awake to light alarming the wall.
"Review, retreat," my dreams tell me
as I wait on the pillow. The parade
of naked emperors will pass again—
the children still asleep upstairs.

Opening the quilts, my skin leaps
past the mirror that stares crazy
out the window at apple trunks.
Nothing flinches as I, naked father,
ride the tense balls of my feet
to the fire. I find it in ash.

In the kitchen, I strip a ripe orange
from Modesto, eat it, shivering.
Across the valley, snow announces
the first blue birds. A thin red line
of blood wants to rise past 40 again.
Coffee's a volcano, the honey's local.

Cats cry hungry at the door. I open to
lions and tigers dwarfed and tame. Did
Nebuchadnezzar throw me in this den?
My feet say "socks." I eat chocolate cake.
Who can argue? Interest is higher now
that it's ever been. I tiptoe back

to the bedroom past the hostages held
by the mad mirror. My wife is asleep.
All night, part of her is listening
for the cries of children or lost mice.
At breakfast, she'll translate nine new
smiles for the dog. I grab my glad rags

in a bunch and run for the shaggy rug.
It is a good day for making cedar doors–
louver by louver. So many scraps need to be
put together. Now I've finished this one.
Light comes through the open spaces here
but always indirectly, and I install no

easy latch for closing.

FOR MY FRIEND
FROM THE CATHERINE CREEK HERONRY

Over me, you sew the sky together, friend.
Crossing the April mountain afternoon that high–
no blue seam shows. Your wings are nothing Herod

understood. In China, I once stood before my frozen
Chinese class and wrote "Hope" on the blackest board
then wrote about you–fishing–in December–

standing on one leg, catching rainbow at the only
open water on a frozen river.
How you skulk along alone, my friend, and thrive!

How your people survived the bloody marketplace–
those plumehunters who tried to kill you all–for
feathers in their hats–a hundred years ago.

Remember those gauche Victorian lovers–of pelf?
At $32 an ounce, they were desperate for grace.
And you were rescued by the refuge of the law.

Your tribe centered this valley, made the world
round enough to be my life. Now every year,
I float my praise under your home–

that habitat of imperfection in the black willow
forks of love. You are shadow, energy, and peace.
In December, I saw your great angelic wings

suddenly flare from the ditch and in that dark,
my courage began to rise again.
Last night, I gave you my right hand in a dream.

My left crossed over to be sure you were alive–
to hold on blind–as I am holding now.
You did not fight. I was not afraid.

Now, I fly with you in this blue montane,
this round interior morning beyond morning.
Where will you take me now–oh great one–

my lover of quiet water and this graceful wind?

THE WETTEST YEAR IN HISTORY

Small rain rights the country green
dissolves the hardened fist of drought
opens up the throats of frogs
releases that good woman–Hope–
to come dibbling among the beds
of tigers in the greening grass again.

Soft rain writes the country green.
Thighs of hikers climb to water drums
new mushrooms–so soft eternal– roll.
Fire meadows and vast mountains flower
flare as bands of sudden rainbow arc across
a changeling sky of fifty different blues.

Complex rain rights the country green.
The ram is shorn, the kestrels scream
starlings from the elm, wheat greens,
mice copulate and multiply like weeds
as fat house cats smile to themselves
the smiles of literal content.

Good rain writes the country green
and everywhere citizens still pretend
some cosmos conspires against them
as they sweat away at some new weed,
thorn, burr, thistles rank on rank
where last year they remember none.

Holy rain will write the country green.
Oasis locust always last to flower.
They wait for June–no matter what syringa do.
Wood houses pray for shade, patience, bark,
new roots, enduring wood. Lost lovers
suck nectar from these dangling creamy

trees in flower, abundance ripening again
within their mouths. Small town rooms lie
wide awake–luminous with gold moons.
Silent bats and soft codling moths begin to fly
the darkness now and one night–unknown–
the great mosquito feast begins.

MEMORIAL DAY, 1994

Quiet cars from town roll up the hill again–
the graves are waiting now–the lawn new-mown–
locust trees all flower–white blossoms
dangling, fine clustering of light,
fragrance branching in the shade–
as people stop, park, and bend before the stones
they love–remembering, remembering.

Many carry two-pound coffee cans
covered with aluminum foil
filled with iris, lilacs, peonies–
whatever grows beside the door
whatever is freely blooming now–
and by the graves they place the coffee cans
add water from the standpipe valve
to keep their gestures living longer than a day.

Then they stand there quiet and survey
what May has brought them to again–
worship, ritual, gaze, pause, death light,
prayer, silence, a name under flowering trees
and beyond them the rows of stars and stripes
sway in wind and ask them to salute
but they turn, start their engines,
drive slow and empty down the hill again

to town, one woman wondering aloud:
"Who will bring flowers to my grave?"
"No one, no one," her sister says.
"We're almost all gone now."
And who will see the locust trees in
their magnificence? I ask myself,
or see the tendrils of blue vetch
weaving deftly through the ditch beside
the road, the bright bachelor buttons in

their polyphony singing wild lights
in barrow pits of love? No one sees them
now. What of the tightest tumult of pods
dangling from green caragana shrubs which
–two weeks ago–were thick with orange
-striped bumblebees staggering with food?

Prepare yourself to be forgotten here–
you who lived just one block away
and watched every Memorial Day–for all
beauty to be seen–as faithful townspeople
drove slowly up the hill with flowers in
their coffee cans–containers they prefer–
so cheap and easy to abandon there
and shining with dead ore from far away.

RUNNING THE EASY WATER

for Alicia and Alex

Our silver canoe slides away on Sunday afternoon.
Catherine carries five of us together–down, down
we meander, fingers in water, fishing short lines.
Your friends stream along, glad to come, to linger.

In the stern, I am your quiet old guide, power,
oarsman, steersman, rudder–cedar in my hands.
David tells a joke. Geese launch their migrant wings
toward grace, their feather robes gliding over us.

Hiding mallards suddenly explode, their orange feet
staggering, dripping up the sky. "Did that scare you?"
"Deer, deer," says a whispering hand. We hush and stare.
The buck is velvet still. You've forgotten who you are.

Under Godley Bridge, we hide. The drowned pig rots.
You talk his stink to death. Colleen says she's lost.
Downstream, you land piratic, tough. Two girls steal
wild iris, camas, swamp lilies in a raid. For love

they stir the anthill to a boil, then shriek and bolt.
A spider decides to stow away. He walks their plank.
Such a heartless crew. Two boys christen shining sticks
for swords. Muskrat disappears. High blooming hawthorn

swallows us alive. At Cove Bridge, your mother is waiting.
We beach in grass together–our safe ending.
You clamber up the bank and disappear. She wants to hear
your story, and you tell her smile everything at once.

I watch you go and start to think. I wait, then call out:
"Will someone help me—with the boat?" How could I be
full all afternoon, then suddenly so empty and drifting
away alone in some solitary slough?

Thanks for coming back. Alone, a father can't always
carry everything from the landing without losing—
losing something

WILDERNESS WALKING SONGS

Eagle Cap

The mountain in Mirror Lake does not waver
in the wind. This means Wallowa calm has come.

Even tons of stone have settled down for a few
million years of sleep. From mistletoe and fir,

shade lulls your eyes. From deep water, your
new face rises slow. Some old grief sinks away.

Wenaha

Now, the meadow opens, the trail becomes
a stroll. Lily, wild rose surround you

everywhere. July afternoon. High blue.
A gray jay glides her soft silent body by.

The river and this ponderosa shade are all.
Come on. Take off your clothes and swim.

Unload that fear you carefully packed in.
Let this river bathe you like a dream.

OPENING DAY

Last night the wind cast gold needles down.
In morning fog, I hunt some gray sudden shape
above lake hills. I am fourteen. I stand
alone and listen. Below the Goat Ranch slopes,
nothing moves.

Thick buck brush below the logging road
slopes into the trees. These mountains
burned the year that I was born. Gold red
sun smoulders the pine horizon east—
over Edgemere way.

This is opening day, October, 1959.
I wait for a mule deer that Idaho promised
was my own. My borrowed boots are tight.
My new red jacket and red felt hat—
gifts old grandfather bought.

The fog and silence? So huge I cannot hear.
Raisins and chocolate in my vest whisper
to me. Mt. Spokane? Too far away to see.
I stand silent, open, waiting. I want any
wild life to move.

Nothing does. I take another step into that
mass of fog. An old rifle leads my trembling
hands. My pocket holds a tag I cannot
lose:"You must provide, you must provide."
Wind sends more gold larch needles

ticking down. My ears roar with the morning
I was born. Everyone is hungry and waiting
for me now. My new heart pounds old drums
to make one shot a clean swift kill
to bring my first meat home.

25

AMONG DECOYS

Two wild geese flying internation
wings came soaring down on slow grace
to rest among what seemed their kind
on a remote pond–wilderness listening around.

Decoys bobbed neat wooden heads and bills
when those geese splashed in. No eyelid
moved. Their random bodies seemed alive,
a refuge, a community at ease, at home.

Perfectly deceived, those two wild birds
let their bilingual billing gabble on
and on, their migratory music be silence
articulate between themselves. They fed on secrets

in the marsh, dove for dreams, loved October
–echoing–and mountains flaring gold fire
around. When decoys did not answer, those
wild birds began to wonder if the locals

were just polite?–maybe just demure?–
maybe mute?–maybe souls at peace?–
wild geese pinioned each possibility aloud.
As blue, then gray, then no light fell,

the decoys held their painted faces smart.
All night, their perfect wings were still–
their carved silence absolute, invulnerable.
At dawn, as two wild geese rowed softly upward

through late stars, calculating guns began
to fire from public blinds where those
decoy makers concealed their careful aims.
Wild blood turned that pond incarnadine.

The decoys stared their usual fake stares
of perfect, empty, and deceptive selves
and they nodded on and on and on.
They had done their jobs–such good actors–

poseurs all dumb, deaf, mindless, blind–
ideal shapes advertising an illusion–
perfect–for making
a killing–

IN THE TIME OF GOLD TREES

The doe comes down carefully to kale.
In the dark, she comes nibbling
so quiet the dog doesn't hear–
thief, lover, dreamer, ghost.
It is late November now–too late
to change–too late–
the kale so green, so rich that
snow cannot touch its potency.
How did she know it was time?

The doe comes down for kale.
In the morning, half the leaves
are gone. Nothing but her perfect
tracks are left for me to taste–
those triangles in my soil
that will never disappear.
How did she know I grew this ripeness here?
How did she discern such vulnerability?
I'm forty eight this fall.

The doe comes down at dark for kale.
I shout. She runs. I think of poaching
her sweet steaks–meat close to home.
"There is a doe eating the kale,"
I tell my wife. "Don't kill her,"
she says. So, she will continue
to take my garden to Glass Mountain.
Half of my row is there now–
half of my life gone–
Why did she come this year? Why now?

Why is she made of fire?

EXCUSES IN SNOW

The morning of deep snow I, being lost
as usual after early class, wandered out to study
the white tons fallen overnight–new, silent, absolute.
Breathing in the frozen air as though I were
some explorer staggering toward a pole
living some discovery I had to know, I stood
on icy treacherous steps of stone and stared
as snow plows arranged this storm in berms.
As I waited there, an older student came to me:

"Sorry to be late today. The blind calf came
through our fence again. I had to get her in.
The neighbors were gone. She might have died
if I hadn't stayed." I turned to her–fifty, stocky
bright, fair–she lived a farm far out of town.
"Blind calf? How can this be?" I asked.
"Why they keep her–I don't know," she said
"I put her in the pen with our blind cow. "
"Blind cow?" I asked again.
"I don't know why we keep her either."
"Black Angus?" I asked.
"Yes," she said.
"A blind black calf lost in two feet of snow–
how does it find its way?" I asked incredulous.
She stared at me. She didn't know the continent
where I stood–thirty years of teaching gone
my head a private blizzard of its own.
"It must know where feed and water are," she said.
"At your barn?" I asked.
"Yes," she said, "that's where the calf always comes.
What did I miss?" she asked.

"Let's go in," I said and walked with her–hot coffee in
the union waiting, attendance drifting beyond control–
all late too late life excused again–by storm.

29

II.

INTERIOR COLUMBIA:
IN AND OUT OF TOWNS

DOWN THE COLFAX GRADE

June, 1996

Loaded with grandfather's midnight hives
our Chevy truck roared against the weight
of honeybees pushing us too fast
down grade. I was twelve that June, 1955.

"Whitman's the richest county in America,"
my grandfather said and pumped the brakes
hard to keep us legal, to keep the truck from
blowing up, to keep awake as we came down

to buggy garish lights. Our eighty swarms–
lashed with hemp rope in complex knots–
flashed white angles across the black windows
of main street, then we climbed out of Colfax

to soft ruts of dust and barbed gates of
sweetclover fields where swales, full moon,
and owls welcomed us. "Palouse," they said,
"Palouse," and by their light, we settled

each queenly colony on King's native grass.
When the rows of white hives were parallels–
entrances turned east for sunrise light–
we opened each furious brood and fled as bees

boiled out to sting us anywhere they could–
inside our pants, armpits, nostrils, ears.
As the moon went down, we parked in green pasture
rolled out sleeping bags on the empty truck

slept there together under the Great Dipper—
one life ending, another beginning. At sunrise,
we drove down to Colfax for strange hotcakes,
then rolled three hundred miles home in sweat.

Today, alone, I coast down this Colfax grade—
loaded with the summers I was given here
forty years ago—a gift only lotus eaters know:
hot August days sweating and stealing tons

of waterclear honey, days granted to a boy
of twelve and his grandfather—two Georges
far from home. In these eroding hills, we
found abundance—enough to make grandfather

cry out with cramps in his heavy hands—
and we did not degrade the loam.

THE BLACK WOLF OF LOVE

This landowner thinks he's rich
but weeds lord all his ground.
They carry me—cheat and foxtail—
over his broken stile.

In the fallow field, I hear
the property belongs to banks.
The tenant farmer's dog comes out
then stalks my tracks.

This pasture's owned by Widow Jean
whose perfect yard I mark.
Her grass I call a Mushroom Town.
For mayor, I nominate the moon.

Across the road, I walk the freehold
of the Church. They built
this fort for God's Indian trade.
The factor calls me Skulk.

Over another fence, I'm on open land
owned by creeks and meadowlarks,
hawks and wind. Each sound is a deed.
Their courthouse is my ear.

Vaulting the chain link fence,
I fall into the library of death.
The grass is mowed. Plastics flinch
by the stone books holding breath

as I pass. Now seventh is the state.
The field's open, tilted, green.
Harvest here is balls and bats
and childrens' screams.

I steal my shadow over this trail.
Trespass is my name.
I am the black wolf of love.
Nothing is mine. I just go around.

GYPPO

Old Joe Padgett ran a lumber mill
sawing Hoodoo pine out Blanchard way.
One Sunday night in Spirit Lake–
our hymns, prayers, testimonies,

my stepfather's preaching all done
again–Joe held up his right hand.
"See that, boy?" he said to me.
"That taught me patience, so–

let that be a lesson to you now."
In that cold sanctuary, I stared
and stared. His thumb was gone.
Then he shook my hand, his stub

of bone and iron fingers gripped
like God. My face turned red.
I was twelve that year and new
in Idaho. Joe Padgett's voice

burned with wilderness that night
forty years ago. Why can I not
not not forget?

PASSING THE VIOLINIST'S HOUSE: A POEM
IN MEMORY OF C. ROBERT GROTH (1930-1987)

(502 6th Street, La Grande)

Imagine this April mountain morning–
sudden snow and sun glazing the new crocus–
the one story house of the dead professor–
C. Robert Groth, the concertmaster of La Grande–
where serious art is merely entertainment news.
Imagine Dr. Groth riding the edge of his chair
like a high hurdler when he played pizzicato–
Imagine why he smoked his lungs black by fifty five–

A newsprint flag flies hard, faded, flat
in his window now. He believed in soldiers.
He was a veteran of foreign war and Army bands.
Red tulips his peaceful wife planted
cringe in red silence under snow by their door.
She survived him, taught oboe
all those years, her reedy tolerance still
a pure fermata on his self-inflicted end.
Their lawn is plain and flat as boredom.
Their Volvo's disappeared–
his tweed jackets and tuxedos all gone to second hand.

He used to stand and smoke on granite
steps, the northwest portico of Inlow Hall,
under that quote from Cicero. He'd suck in
some smoke, then loudly hiss it out as
though he were a dragon, as though he needed
to show the gold pride in his teeth–
his hitched-up gray slacks a little short–
his dark socks a little slack–
his tie and white shirt military neat.
They said he always came to work at eight
walked home for lunch like a Swiss clock
always left at five to read his news.

Dutiful and talented–the chairman said–
the kind of man every music faculty wanted–
though rumor said he might have kept someone
in his music cabinet–under the Schubert sonatas.

Walking by his common house in this late snow,
an ugly gray terrier named Doubt–
who lives here now–comes out to snarl.
Don't think of Groth's shining violin, no,
nor his habituated self-destructive hand, no,
nor Claus–his first name he never used–
no, nor the concertos he played appassionata.
Some simple justice for him is all you owe.
Just remember that story he told once–

how one year, deciding to finish his
doctorate, the highest note and so the most
dangerous degree, C. Robert went to
Eugene and studied there. Ah, university!
He performed with all the best orchestras,
chamber groups, conductors, and wanted to
stay there, but he had to return to La Grande–
where serious art is merely entertainment news.

The first day back, he heard what was wrong,
what was really wrong, what he had heard before but
not been able to identify: every instrument,
every piano, the whole community of instruments–
all half a tone flat.

Setting out to re-tune every string around him,
some people thought he was crazy then–
the sole violinist in a town of fiddlers–
the only perfect pitch among rusted tuning forks–
the new professor with his new degree–
why didn't he hear this before?
Why did he want everything changed now?
Was that half a tone flat the force that fed

38

the endless cigarettes into his mouth–
blacked his lungs–so black he could
not play another bar? Was it the wilderness
around him? Leaking roof? Dead old concert hall?
Memory of war? Those efficient petty
and perfidious deans wanting to be shouted down?
The zero love? That new young pianist too talented?
The fate of being remote and bozos at the door?
And then to find out–he seemed to be the only
ear who could hear a 440 "C"?

You tell me.
At the college where C. Robert Groth taught
his fate too many years, they unveiled
new mascots today: male and female cartoons
drawn by ArtFarm Smith from Portland–
caricatures of short primitive people
carrying sticks and acting crazy,
bones in their hair, four-fingered, ignorant,
violent. The president, the dean of students,
the student body president, and the eight
committee members–including two professors–
all pretended they had just unveiled
something magnificent paid for with real
money and served with sweet dangerous cake–
now nothing but crumbs. I went. I saw them all–

and the newspaper carried the big story
of the celebration and published the cartoons–
as though slick superficial images are some
kind of perfection, as though ugliness were just
a matter of entertainment news, as though
stereotypes don't kill us all.

MY STUDENT–OLDER THAN AVERAGE

Prospector with no mine–
away for twenty years–
suddenly saw himself as
gold flake sinking alone

in the sand by the river.
So he came to school again
to reclaim his life.
Grubstake, he wanted,

one easy winter, a girl
for company, he said–
some of that mother lode
to warm his empty

bed. He believed his nuggets
glowed at night, believed
in thieves and Midas luck.
Panning Geology, he said

he'd seen all that before
it got into a book.
In tough assays, he told me
he'd abandoned all his claims

to hunt for gold that's pure–
gold free from tons of stone.
I eased him with Incomplete
in everything I could–

Spring Quarter, he was gone.
Somewhere down a mineshaft now
he's blasting another face,
following another vein–

more tailings—
more Oregon—
more coarse ore—
so much to refine.

SAFEWAY CONVERSATION

Give me an apple with a worm–
I want mine perfect red.

They cost too many poison deaths.
I want that paradise.

A simple knife can cut it–
I want sweetness to the core.

Besides, these worms repulse me.
I'd feed them to the horse.

How can you stand the way they–
I try to be myself.

Please, a pound of those Delicious
Stay away from me.

But I can't change overnight.
Watch out for your hair.

DIALOGUE AT BUCKHORN LOOKOUT

(read for the 10th anniversary celebration of the Hells
Canyon National Recreation Area, June 30,1985)

Thousands of us, thirty years,
a boxcar of testimony–to save you
from obscenity. We've come back today
to find you, to remember.

My life is old.
I could have held you all, then forgot.
My grass is infinite in morning light.
My water is sure. I am living, still.

Do you remember the hearings
the committees, the hours of testimony
the nights on phones, in offices, in rooms–
Idaho, Oregon, Washington, D.C.?

I attend my own–the shadows by elder
berries in August, the eagle feather
floating down ten thousand feet. I hold
out the meeting of wren and old basalt.

But great men helped us. Do you remember them?
William O. Douglas fooled the powerful
with his test–so simple–of real, public
interest to save you from–

Did he ever stay with me? I am massive
steep, and vast. I am delicate and huge.
Many have opened me and taken something.
Is this why you have come?

Do you remember Senator Packwood?
He was the man from Oregon who pledged
that what happened in the East would not
happen here–a brilliant champion.

Beaver may have said his name to me.
Look around you: I contain multitudes.
Forgive me. Names are lost here. I am
endless congress too infinite for words.

But Brock Evans, Jerry Jayne, John Barker,
Pete Henault, Floyd Harvey, Dale Storey,
and many more sweat nights and days
to save you–

They are saving themselves. I am
their peace, their beauty in the world.
I have washed their agonies in cold water
and given them back as dreams. Were they proud?

No. Voices go soft here around a fire.
So much had to be opposed.
They burned Floyd Harvey's camp to ash
and Packwood had to go around the rules.

Did they wake early enough to see
the first light sting my west rim gold?
Did they admire my snakes, yellowjackets,
my hawthorne, my augustan sun?

At first, it seemed hopeless. Idaho Power
and the Corp of Engineers had begun to
plan your death before many of us were born.
How could we have been ready?

My water moves the rock. My sturgeon swallow
anything and thrive. I have a great heart
for returning fish, but many never come back.
The biggest ones are deep and old.

How did we know we would be like Joseph–
fighting far authority for native beauty
like Tohoolhoolzote–fighting armies of
uniformed, well-armed lies?

Creeks come to me full and brown in spring.
My slopes and ridges bloom when you are
still freezing in town. I have starved you
down to horsemeat, sunk your boats, your lives.

The power companies snorted and stamped
and paid big salaries, but we were hammering
the steel ring of law for their nostrils.
The vote was 342-53. Symms couldn't stop us.

Do not trouble me. I can rock you dead
with one simple stone. I forget everything.
I forget nothing. Now do you hear my trees
listening? They are dreaming of eternity.

Why do you seem to forget us? We gave years
to keep the cement bones out of your throat.
You should know us. We are the tribe that
refuses to mark you. We've come back today.

Enough now. Be still. My singing
surrounds you–deep, fragile, far. Listen.
My life is old. I hold you all as grass.
Now let me be alone. I have spoken.

COYOTE CREATES YELLOWJACKET
FROM THE BONES OF JOB

Coyote and Mrs. Raven were roasting fat bear steaks over the fire at Five Points Creek. They watched as the White people dragged their wagons up the rocky ridges and through the lodgepole thickets of the Cayuse people. After the wagon train passed, they saw a bony old man with big white teeth and a white beard and bloodshot eyes and hands like claws. He was staggering and stumbling along through the trees. He was starving and carrying a Bible and mumbling "Error's Chain, Error's Chain, Error's Chain."

"Hey, you lost?" Mrs. Raven waved her wing. Coyote saw the old man was covered with scars and scabs. He was wearing a sackcloth dipped in ashes. Without being invited, the old man ate a chunk of bear meat and smacked his lips.
"What's your name?" Coyote said.
"I'm Job, the good man God made to suffer–just to see how much pain I could take before I changed gods."
"Was he into sado-masochism or something?" Coyote said. Again without being invited, Job took two chunks of bear meat and wolfed them down. He gave a loud belch.
"Why you coming to Oregon?" Mrs. Raven said.
"These White people are trying to escape from suffering in Oregon. We just can't have that. People here got to suffer as bad as people anywhere else, so I'm hauling West all the Historical Suffering I can carry and spreading it around." Job laughed and pointed his bony finger back at the thousands of Indian and White graves along the Oregon Trail. When Job thought Coyote wasn't looking, he stole another chunk of bear meat.
"You *like* to make people suffer?" Coyote said angrily.
"Does black book make you do it?" Mrs. Raven pointed at Job's Bible with her impeccable, black shining wing.
"Me and God and the Devil collaborate," Job boasted. "These people are dreaming of Eden, and if you'll bear with me, we're giving them pure Hell." He cackled high–through his nose. With pure impunity, Job swallowed the last juicy chunk of bear–swallowed it whole, then stared at Coyote and Mrs. Raven just

like a hungry dog.

"Grab this greedy sadistic fool," Coyote shouted to Mrs. Raven, "before he eats us too." They threw that Old Testy Job into the fire where–poof–he turned into white smoke and black ashes–and the five pieces of juicy bear meat were broiling on the fire again–as though they'd never been eaten, as though Job had been just a ghostly idea.

"Now what you going to do with this mess?" Mrs. Raven asked. She was always cleaning up after him, it seemed.

"I have to invent something for these people," Coyote said. He took an obsidian flake from Glass Butte, a drop of venom from Rattlesnake, some fine soft gold from Snake River, and he mixed them all up with the ashes of Job and said a word and sang a Cayuse song and Yellowjacket arose on glistening wings from the fire and began to fly in slow circles around Coyote's head.

"Ha," said Mrs. Raven, "you'll be sorry you made that thing."

"It's better than Job," Coyote said. Yellowjacket flew closer to Coyote's nose and stung him right between the eyes. "Hey, that hurt," Coyote cried. "Go get a job or something." Coyote's eyes were starting to swell shut and just then Yellowjacket stung him again–on the nose. Mrs. Raven flew off laughing on her big soft wings. How you going to teach him anything? Coyote dove deep into Five Points Creek and stayed under water and soaked his swollen face. When it was dark, he ran up in the highest mountains where Yellowjacket could not find him.

See, Coyote knew that Old Man Job was really a powerful cannibal, so Coyote burned that historical disguise by throwing Job in the fire and made Yellowjacket–who has no disguises, and who can put a little suffering in any day, but not too much to bear. This is why, in Oregon, people believed there should not be as much Historical Suffering as there is in other places, but Yellowjacket still stings people here without apology and carries off little chunks of their meat without asking–just like Old Man Job did that day. Mrs. Raven is still scolding him and cleaning up everything.

A HANFORD VETERAN: JAY MULLEN'S STORY

From Missouri, we moved to Spirit Lake in 1944.
My father was stationed on Lake Pend Oreille.
He wanted us to be together there.
He wanted to fight to save his family.
He thought we would be safe with him

in Idaho. Then one day when I was five
all my hair just turned white, fell out—
the whole school itching—eyes burning—
we didn't know why. We were kids living
in Idaho where we were safe from war.

It took fifteen years for that iodine-131
to gather in my throat—my thyroid—here—
he pointed to his neck—and when it did,
I was deathly sick. At 19 and dying—
I promised God that if I got over this—

I would go anywhere he wanted me. Later, I
went to Africa on a mission for ten years
then came back to Spirit Lake, Idaho, again.
The Presbyterian Church we believed was
still there but lots of things had changed.

My father supported the atom bomb on Japan.
He would have been the first wave
of troops ashore. He was sure we were safe
in Spirit Lake—he would have done anything
to protect us—you know—

and there we were—being destroyed by
the same radiation that was protecting him,
and there we were—in Idaho—of all places—
becoming victims of the same thing
that killed thousands of Japanese

and there we were–sure our parents were
doing everything they could to protect us
but they could not protect us from Hanford's
secret experiments in power. I'm sorry.
I can't tell it without crying now.

ON BURNSIDE

She tried her thumb against the rip
of traffic that drunk Friday night.
I walked by, sealed against desire,
telling myself I had no car.

Helpless in a block, I turned, went
back, asked if I could, somehow, help.
"See that damn duffel?" she said.
Together, we pulled for a yellow sign.

"At sea, I could save your life,"
she said, "but on land I'm lost."
Scars on scars told more–a flat
dangerous world she sailed.

I left her at the Sea and Land
where she told me, "Tonight, by god,
I won't be no whore." Late, late
in my hotel, loud sirens kept me

waking over and over to sea roar.

THE ENDING OF THOMAS JEFFERSON, YEOMAN FARMER

(in auctioneer style)

Maybe he bought out the North American Elk Breeders
Association Convention in Billings, Montana

or maybe the Bosque Valley Ranch and Oak Bluff
Ranch Boer Goat Sale offering 60 head

or maybe he hit that American Sheep Industry Convention
or maybe the Farm Forum at Shelby High School Gym

or maybe he got to the California Farm Equipment Show
and International Exposition in Tulare

or the National Corn Growers Association Corn Classic
or the North American Deer Farmers' Conference this year

in Nashville, Tennessee, or the Annual Meeting of
the National Potato Promotion Board in Denver

or maybe he got took at the Treasure State Auction in Conrad
or maybe the World Beef Exposition in Madison, Wisconsin

or maybe the Way Out West Bird Expo where he bought
everything from finches to macaws, cages, feed,

or maybe the Diamond V Ranch Annual Bull Sale in Wibaux
or Johnson's Black Simmental Ranch Sale in Baker

or maybe RX Cattle Co Red Angus Roundup Bull Sale in Russell
or maybe Johnson's Black Simmental Ranch Sale in Burley

or maybe Shield Bar Herefords on the Little Missouri
or maybe Wildcat Ruby Red Devon Ranch Production Sale

or maybe Dusty Prairie Ranch American Bull and Female Sale
or maybe the Clear to the Bone Production Sale

or maybe Duprel Charolais Ranch 19th Annual Bull Sale in Vale
and if he had anything left, well, he by god might have

listed his beefalo with the American Beefalo World Registery
as long as his beefalo were 3/8ths bison and 5/8ths bovine

or he might have gone off with Mardi Linhart who loves her cows
so much that she's now touring as Montana Angus Queen

or he might have bought ostriches from Northern Tier because this
industry is not a fad and birds have microchipped ID

or he might have bought into the Emu Prime Processors business
with the New Breed Emu Ranch now taking slaughter contracts

or he might have bought a used tractor from the Machine Shed in
Kansas or Colorado from friendly dealers with free numbers

or he might have become a woman in agriculture and maybe got
beat up by a bull or kicked by a drunk horse

or maybe he sold his trees for top prices to Brand S Lumber
who buys standing timber and environmental forestry

or bought some Australian export beef and watched it fall
by 90,000 tons as 1.4 million cattle die in the drought

or earned $5.44 an hour in 1994 compared with
$5.82 an hour in 1993 as a Montana farm worker

or maybe he no-till planted his last nickel on 4.2 million acres when
he could have plowed the old way on 3.5 million acres

or maybe he developed a test to detect liver fluke in
cattle, sheep, and goats at Montana State

or bought that new mounted press wheel system for
the 820 Precision Tillage Tool from Flexi-coil

or called the One to One Introductions Service in Billings,
Montana, who helped him decide–in this marketplace–where to

meet someone to love or maybe he bought what true cattlemen
look for–bull semen from the LRA Rosebud Rope 390 whose

semen is just $15 per straw–calves balanced in all traits or
maybe he tried that Elk Breeders Convention again

where Baxter Black takes the art of rhyme one step further with
his lunatic wit and animated delivery with everything from

parasites to postmortems, and if he didn't get there maybe he
cleaned up his oil spill with wool blankets because wool can

absorb 10 to 30 times its weight in oil while still repelling water,
or maybe he bought some yaks, the massive, wooly

rarest, and least studied cattle on earth, straight from the herd
at the Toronto Zoo, or maybe he died wondering why bats are

the farmers' best friends and we know so little about them, or
maybe he lost his shirt on that first commercial winter wheat

called Halt because it resists the Russian wheat aphid that
came out three years ahead of schedule, and that voracious little

insect cost Colorado wheat growers $12.1 million in direct losses
in 1994 and led to $17.7 million in indirect losses

or maybe he got his pesticide applicator's license
or bought that video on "Keeping Nature in Balance" by

Jay Novacek of the World Champion Dallas Cowboys
or maybe he bought some recycled plastic sheets from Coon

Manufacturing in Spickard, Missouri, where the company
gives customers a good price or maybe he turned into a well driller,

or a fence builder or a feedyard manager or an animal poisoner,
or a weed killer, or maybe bought some Friesian cattle for

his herd, or got himself all wrapped up in an all-steel
Mr. Cowman horse barn and riding arena, or got a

Governor's Award, or a Beef or Pork Industry Scholarship
or bought himself some custom boots made just perfectly

for his feet from Kathy Schultz in Mosca, Colorado, who's been
making them for 30 years, or maybe he got disaster relief for his

weather damaged crops or got electrocuted by his grain
auger or got his transmission fixed or got himself some survival

blankets for calves, and then he needed some stirrup buckles out of
stainless steel and heat-treated aluminum and he needed to

buy some real Texas longhorns and revolutionary water tanks and
then he got into technical agriculture and progressive beef cattle

and black sheep to register and crossbreeding guides
for the western range and metal ear tags and horses, yes, horses

from the TJ Bar Ranch called "Sail on Priest" and "Azure Te Speed"
and "Jeopardy Rocket" and he bet his farm loan on a race now that

the lottery adjusted his expectations to $16,000,000 bucks
and in the end, he found out that the U.S. right now,

the U.S. has the fewest number of farms in 140 years and maybe
he just sold the whole shootin' match to the realtors at Trendmaker

and moved his broke ass to town, by god, just like everybody else.

ROAN FILLY

And don't forget now: that roan
filly you saw just once up Grass Valley–
damn, she was a beauty–damn, her
haunches just turned you to jelly–
crazy proud she was–all sashay and prance–
and when she ran, damn if the sweet
April air didn't burn blue tongues of fire
around her wild strawberry hide–damn
she was too fast, too hot, too smart
to ever be bridled, broke, or caught.

That only time, she bolted sudden
down the ridge like grass fire in wind
like she dared you just to watch her
run, like she dared you just to even
see her withers, fetlocks, or flanks
dance, like she was some red dust
devil, some heat lightening you could never
touch–damn–and she just jumped that
old flimsy fence, reared, squealed,
farted, spun, took off again–eyes burning
that dark red–like cougar eyes at night–
her mane a flaming mass, her tail out,
back straight, strong, her chest too deep
for words. What could you say or do?

By that old fence, you stood dumbfounded
staring at those deep prints her curves cut
in your turf, your life torn to open pulp.
Christ, was that roan a horse or what!

What became of that filly I still wonder now.
Probably got her wild ass hauled off to town–
that Redmond yard where they ship horsemeat
to France still buys a lot of head for slaughter.
Christ, what a waste, I say,
Christ, what a waste!

A. J. DICKEY COULDN'T RUN THE ENDS

for Alva J. Dickey (1937-1997)

bronze October afternoons we played flag
in the park, so he always hiked—our center
until "Statue of Liberty" was called
so he could be a back. He loved that pose,
waiting to fool everyone with fakes
just before his big brown boots began

to cut the turf with his halt steps.
A.J. Dickey couldn't rock those pink-
sweatered nights in gyms of Elvis girls
but he always sang good bass in choir.
Four years we were the back row boys
in jeans, sang blues for school,

Jesus hymns and choruses for God
and holding the last notes of songs,
A.J. would look at me and I at him.
We wondered who would be the first
to breathe. Our voices trembled with vibrato
under flannel shirts and common robes.

A.J. Dickey could not play the floor
or crash the field where good legs ran,
so his blue pen kept every score, his
good hands ran the dying clock
on the gymnasium wall. He hustled
towels, basketballs, and tape, rode

the bus and bench with Coach Butler
every game, came home to frozen midnight
with the team. I still see his careful gait—
short step, short slide, short step—
down Spirit Lake's ice streets.
A.J. had his beat, knew how to fall,

58

how to heave himself back up.
He knew balance was delicate to keep.
More than once his brother Jim had to
give A.J. his own hands, heart, legs
and arms. We were all the same.
Bright birth flawed us all–somehow.

A.J. was our center–
the first to comprehend.

III.

SEGUES FOR INTERSTATE 84

SEGUES FOR INTERSTATE 84

Meacham
is married ravens bowing to the roadkill deer. They
peck and waddle through their morning devotions
keeping the immortal circle moving through the sky.
These are the forests where illusions burn.
Eighty years, men fought native fire as enemy
then learned she was their only healing friend and

Spring Creek
is the hill where a woman buried her
new born baby under stones. Her husband cracked
his ox whip and hid behind his mask of beard.
With dirty hands, she wiped her tears.
The dream of settlement smeared the page.
Her ghost is still here–protesting this
hard broken country all set on edge.
Children repair her stream while–year after year–

Holdman
grows a white new-painted sign. Now a formal label
in the field announces "WINTER CANOLA" to everyone.
This is new *rape seed* flowering yellow for oil.
Someone keeps our language safe and marketable–
as usual–even in the middle of an empty county.
Latin saves us again from thinking definite things like

Pendleton
where big red letters–PG or PGG–ride the plains and
pregnant river hills. The abandoned drive-in
east of town welcomes you, the billboard empty
now of all desire, and Theater Road is weedy
peace. Under bridges, the Umatilla River curves
cold and blue past the dead sawmill. Last year,
the hospital became a prison where chain links

gleam and concertina wire plays a wounded blues:
"Oh baby, nobody escapes from these places,
  baby, nobody gets through two fences" for

Rew
where blue pigeons perch on the henhouse ridge
above the elevator. Their work is praying that
this forever wind will not blow their dusty plain
all to hell some day. All directions, wheatland is
naked, standard, private–monoculture built by
markets traded lustily–Tokyo to New York.
When men plow the wind, this dust can kill.
These blue pigeons pray for rain in

Stanfield
where the sign says "HOME OF THE TIGERS" but
only brown tumbleweeds growl and stack silently
against the freeway fence. Over them, one kestrel
winnows the morning median, hunts a minion mouse.
See? Everything wants breakfast and where
is the poet Gerard Manley Hopkins today?
His holy dapple dawn-drawn falcon dives–
here–
now
at

Boardman
because pylons are profane. These giant skeletons of
steel take the river's power, march off across
the desert for the Willamette, their fists fat with
electricity, their bodies headless, rigid, juiced.
No one dares call them *drug lords* or *pushers* or kilowatts
a *fix* or outlets a *local dealer* selling pure addiction
to deadly consumption–not yet, not in

Arlington
symbolized by "A." Who remembers the old rivertown
where steamboats used to dock and ferries cross?
The alphabet now arrives in twenty-ton Gray trucks
hauling the steady garbage stream upriver from Portland
and long trains roll down daily–wasted from Seattle.
Here, the first great interior dumping ground that
saves those coastal cities from themselves.
They call it "sanitary" to dignify such lust.
The sign does not say "SEATTLE/PORTLAND LANDFILL--
TONS OF IGNORANCE PER DAY BURIED FOR YOUR
PLEASURE." The "A" on the hill is whitewashed too.
It should be painted red and not like

Woelpern Ranch
this isolate, where white shouts at the gate,
"We're here, we're home, come in, come on."
"NO RETURN TO FREEWAY EASTBOUND" says the sign.
The ridge is a jawbone that opens to the sky.
This basalt watched Joseph ride downriver and
now, industrial wind scatters children far
and another outpost of progress turns marginal
grows doubt, folly, grief, dispossession, fear unlike

The John Day River
lichen who crave these palisades.
There are enough berets of sod
to represent the south of France.
Red and yellow masses paint the cliffs
for miles, and talus slopes arrange
the hard centuries of breakage into
angles of repose. Sometimes, an artist
named Falling Rock gets to the river–
across this easy grade you ride where
lichen crave these palisades beyond

Blaylock Canyon
angling to the water. Now, is the rim Missoula flood?
Ramparts in old wars? Old gods? Nothing fits.
The rhythmic silence of basalt repeats
the rock dove's echoing echoing cry.
Now, send your smartest Faust. Tell him
to count and name every fissure here in
one square mile of stone; write his report
on infinity–before he dies in

Maryhill
at the museum. Now, no Mary here.
The highway railroad baron–Hill–is dead.
The river turned out not to be the Rhine
and lovers left this mansion for the south.
All night now, chess men by the hundreds
checkmate themselves with subtle moves
as petroglyphs in basement rooms beat drums
and sing for salmon and Klickitat fishermen.
Every morning, the curator must build again
her imported empire of belief around Rodin,
around some Romanian queen's silk gown.
Two red hawks ride the centuries of wind
and paper airplane contests win respect–
beauty institutionalized and this remote
requires any cent or light. Below this art,
sweet Takahashi peaches ripen in

Hood River
sun. Wind changed the water here to cash
when the fish were gone.
Now, butterflies with rich nylon wings
spawn across the espresso river.
Hispanic hands pick your apples,
pears, and cherries by the ton.

Issei leave behind the memory of war
their stolen orchards
the memory of being given
their own fruit to eat while
prisoners on racist relocation trains.
One white mountain still attempts
to be silent and above it all
by sending down

Multnomah Falls
sending white water birds diving down
down into the foaming pool.
These never die. Their wings forever
curved with their descending,
they rise, disappear, then
dive down and down again.
and then ascend again anew.
Come clear to me, mountain water
birds, come clear to me again.
I am always listening for
your parallactic cry above

Bonneville
where tons of soft interior wheat slide down the watery
stairway for Asia—noodles for China
by the hundred thousand bushel ride easy—
the barges' white giant letters shouting
"TIDEWATER" and "SHAVER."
Fortunes are made here on the surface while
under water, the spawning chinook circle
and die of hunger. No current carries the odor
of home, no hint of hope to follow.
Here, Woody Guthrie sang his great ironic song
"Roll on Columbia, roll on," while the gates
of dam locked the native river to the treadmill
turbines and their endless civilizing spin.

IV.

VOICE LESSONS IN HELLS CANYON

TRYING OUT

Backstage with your selves
it's riot. You let the house
lights fall and send your cast
of other lives into tableau.

The bear is here—black, shining
in the center lights, blinded
sure of strength, endurance,
voice, and appetites.

Two kids sneak by him easy
to the edge of shade and camp.
A carpenter and his wife lie
naked on their patchy quilts.

Three guerillas take up bows
to guard an old slow farmer
opening his hive of bees beside
a garden`s flowering rank trees.

A blonde girl, haunted, rides
her white horse out of wings;
behind her comes a ragged man
with axe, book, rod, and worms.

He sees the whole stage flash
then bolts. You catch him
at the door and tell him
"No one's here but you," so

he returns to cast his line
through your primordial show.
Last, an old woman walks on
picking blackberries by the gallon

humming to herself, her fingers
stained purple, her bucket half full.
Seeing her, the bear, holding
his nostrils high, his head swaying,

rises. You stand there–helpless–
a stage Johnny–with briars in
your hands. Every self is still.
A heavy curtain opens to applause.

The house is waiting, full, and still.
Your tableau is gone.

A FATHER SPEAKS TO HIS SON
THE ONLY BOY IN THE 7TH GRADE CHOIR

Let me hear you.

You won't always be surrounded by
those forty-seven gigantic girls
wobbling over you on pretending heels.

Forget your sweating hands, your crotch
where jockey shorts insist you scratch.
Let me hear you sing. Lift your chin.

Just think your breath below your waist.
Try not to worry about your hair.
The song is what we came to hear

so give yourself to each note
sustaining that long phrase.
This easy, two-part melody will change

and you won't always be alto, I guarantee,
so be patient with yourself.
Concentrate on the back row. I'm sorry

your mother's at work again tonight.
Don't let that tie and collar choke you
any more. What tries to keep you from

the sound that is your own–be it school,
parent, team, or town–let them know
you won't be shut up

by any of their champions, big principals,
or degrees of fear. Be a singer, kid.
Let me hear you now. That's good alto.

In a year or two, you'll begin to growl.
There's no disgrace in a changing voice.
You'll be diving then–as you must–

for the bottom of the world.

FABLE FOR AN ARROGANT CENTURY

Mr. Is wanted to be The Boss.
He tricked his brother, Real Smart,
into killing all the Should Row bums
telling Real his gun shot nothing
but noisy objective blanks.

Real Smart got excited. He and Is
sold a hundred tickets to a lynching
they planned in the woods. Mrs. Hightech
came in her black gown. She sold popcorn
while people watched those outlaws

Maybe-The-Kid and his Uncle Seems
get doused with gasoline. Everybody left.
Mr. Is and Real got rich. Science, Inc.
built them an imperial house of cards.
Miss Universe moved in. They had fun.

Everything was perfect until one night
two Indian kids named Wonders and Doubts
started wiggling their ears and singing
in the street. The whole house suddenly
disappeared in an inexplicable smoke.

PROFESSORS–IN THEIR MASKS AS FENCE POSTS

Nothing holds us together
but staples and tension
some stiff chunks of alphabet
at the corners.

Our job is acting afraid
to make exceptions, even
for the shadow of that bull
who might need range.

Split up, shrunk, stuck
in high-paid holes, we wear
old moss caps, pay our dues
to the prevailing weather

and hope the dream deer
will come again tonight
and go easily over
this taut barbaric wire.

THE CAGY LAUREATE OF OREGON

for William Stafford

If this poet were
showing you how to fish,
he would not bait your hook
or tell you which lure or line
he might be using for the big ones
breathing at his feet, and if he did confess,
you should just watch his moves–
the way he breathes and swims.

He might say "Cast out of yourself,"
and then he would watch you
reel in something you had snagged–
anything you did not plan too much is fine.
He might stare into the sacred water
before you for an hour
waiting for you to break
your silence, his silence too.

In that fog, if you asked him,
"Why do you hold your line that way?"
he would only smile.
This indirection is his pure
respect for you, his refusal
to be too clear–his respect for
the mystery we all stand before.
Say nothing to reduce it all.

As the big fish swim around
his feet, you might call them
"Dinner." If you did not ask
too much about technique
or bait or hooks or lures or flies
or lead Hugo nuts and bolts,
he would stand beside you,

and if you got your big one on,
his magic net would suddenly appear.

He would release them all,
call the metaphor all wrong, call
it all a worshiping of death
let the fish all go, become
the plain where you stood together–
the fish applauding there–
the protean quietude in all deep water–
become that world beyond the violence
of rationalistic pose.

Can you see him? See his moves?
The way he breathes and swims?

WILDERNESS MAN IN THE GREAT CITY

I'm nibbling.

Taste that acrid powder in fired weapons
people who explode at every corner.

Taste that raw gasoline on streets
uninsured cars; endless reddish lights.

Taste that blood of freak lane-change wrecks
sudden sirens, the nice lies of a thousand stores,

radios, televisions, newspapers, mouths–
even lies on packages of food.

Taste that greed, rapacity, carnage
the tons of waste and death that Lorca saw.

The stench of Minotaur waits around
the corner. I am always out of yarn.

Every moment seems like some kind of fight.
Is there time to be silent or amazed?

Here, I spit out your urban hook so
perfectly concealed in deadly bait.

I'm not swallowing anything.
Your lost leader's a translucent fake.

STAR

in memory of William Stafford (1914-1993)

Maybe every night a star wakes up
leaves your house and climbs
into the sky to be itself
among the galaxies of prayer.

Maybe when the sun is gold again
that star returns to sleep
somewhere inside your doors–
some blind spot you can never see.

Maybe this creature is with you
there–somehow–say as a mother
spider God made, her web so delicate
we're all caught–shimmering.

Eternity is here sleeping–somewhere–
common and silent. When you dream no one
is looking, eternity escapes again–
subtle, quiet, awake–consumed by light.

Be like that star.

MR. WHINE: A SKETCH

With all his prizes counted
from great blind judges far

from home, Mr. Whine he keep
on picking his self-inflicted

wounds, calling scabs his poems.
"How the gods have wronged me"–

(his tongue destroyed them all.)
"How my love has flown me"–

(before he killed her too.)
How does he manufacture

his grievance into grief, then
make it seem authentic stuff?

Ironic tone? What schmaltz!
A satiric burst? Don't laugh!

Just one whiff is all you need
to sense there's something

adulterated there, some
Bluebeard sophist pose,

some stench beyond the law
and his peers will never tell.

They're his jury, after all–
they're the big time neigh–

and neat moaning is on sale
and self-mockery is gold–

No wonder Mr. Whine gets the grant–
he marches to *de mode*.

POINT GUARD BRINGING THE BALL UP COURT

I go right, feed you this quick
no-look pass inside with my left–
*"The twentieth century has not
been kind to the rural west,"*
says historian Richard White
in his fat–check federal book.

You, reader breaking in the key,
I put that one in your hands
–don't put it on the floor–
just turn and shoot, see if you can draw
the hack foul (I've drawn so many now)
I could if I took that ball in hard

off the drive, double pumping, spinning
like this–they never could stop me
in open court. I had follow through,
finesse, good fakes, quickness, a bag of
stutter steps. Count it. Get back.
Hands up.

Next time, I might go left, come back right.
You may not think I see you there at all
but my peripheral vision is better now–
I don't have to look to see you move
inside–just be breaking for the center
and be ready for the pass–

*"The twentieth century has not
been kind to the rural west,"*
says historian Richard White.
See? Same play twice. Surprise them.
That's how we win when justice is
short and the coach–a red-faced Yankee
god–is shouting from the bench.

POETRY, THAT BANDIT

gets away through Talent, always north of Ashland
jail, walks through the Siskiyou black ridges
burning green again, leaves the scorched logs
of summer wildfire to Eugene truckers
and their silver-hooded ornamental dogs.
In mask, Poetry steals a horse and laughs.

Bareback on Appaloosa truth, that once was
a toy horse in that carousel called Town,
Poetry rides east for the interior: space without
pretense, space where silence hears silence and is
still, where wilderness sends wide rainbows

upward out of stone, where lightening, pine,
basalt, and sky are listening for that horse.
In that canyon called the Snake, Poetry finds miles
of mountain rooms where cheap talk is consumed
by grass or cougar, winter or long and silent light.

Poetry sleeps easy by Hells River under eagle trees.
Spring rain falls. Grass mountains green.
Poetry waits–like an old *tewat* fasting, dreaming–
for a voice from fire, water, wing, willow, wind.
Find her–you civilizing bastards–

find her if you can.

V.

INTO THE PACIFIC

FAMILY SCAVENGER

Believes in refuse and loves junk so much
he haunts the household dumps–attic, cellar,
will, hope chest, cobweb closet, gravestone,
leather album with sepia prints, that barrel
of letters in the ditch in rain–Scavenger
seeks the lost family silence at the heart.

Gathering every artifact in sight–snapshots
box by box, bloody letters from the war,
the diaries of years alone, Bibles by the ton,
ivory razor, tusks, pistols, lockets,
clipped curls, albums, lace, sheet music
of the sea–no song too minor–Scavenger packs

them to his cave. Soon he knocks on your life–
jovial as he tells you why your eyes were born,
tells you Emma Goldstein is your definite ancestor
so you're not all goy, tells you who stole
your name, who cut your childish curls, who
put your life inside these stories he has found–

your great uncle falling backward into the goose
pond before he sailed to America to sober up;
that hateful aunt abandoning her little sister
to housekeeping while she enjoyed a pious year
at midwest Bible school; your carpenter grandfather
kicked out of the church he built; your uncle

crippled for life when a school teacher jilted
him, eloped with her student lover to California;
your Scots grandfather a Grenadier in bearskin hat
guarding the bier of Queen Victoria all night;
crossing America in boxcars come your pious aunts;
grandmother comes a child through Ellis Island gates;

84

your dead cousins pose with their cougar hounds;
your German ancestors chop undercuts in trees
so huge that trees became their enemies to burn,
and cedar was the only gold they knew for years.
When Scavenger leaves, your room reeks the salt
sweet sweat memory of love and ghost and give.

You can never be alone in America again.
The silent lost lives in your bones have come
to sound. Your mouth begins to sing some song
you do not know, some pent crude music
you cannot understand but always hear, some five
piece ensemble beating in your ear.

THE TREEHOUSE AT 316 NORTH REGENT STREET, BURLINGTON, WASHINGTON

for my brother Douglas

Remember that great English walnut tree
curving over us, huge shelter in soft green
shade? Remember our treehouse there–that
refuge two boys built of third-grade scraps?

New stepsons then of Rev. Venn, we plied
and played those old boards into a roof
that didn't leak in rain. We munched sardines
and crackers there, prattled our Pig Latin

on the tincan telephone. Remember? You taught
me how to climb up: stand on the garbage can,
raise both hands, lock them tight around
the first branch, then hanging upside down,

throw one leg over the limb and swing yourself
upright. Our treehouse was too high for adult
righteousness to reach–we kept silence about that–
and we sat too quietly to be caught reading

those banned and sinful comic books–
Superman, Batman, Bugs Bunny, Red Ryder–
secret gifts from our kick-the-can friends
like Frankie Younger, Dave Wollen, Ida June.

Remember how those taboo pages stained
our fingers? We would hide those pulpy heroes
in our secret place–the damp tree crotch
under the floor–just above the reach of

that hardwood stick with which new
Stepfather beat our hands red with pain
if we did not eat every bite of liver or
corn soup by the time he set on the clock.

Remember that stiff self-righteous stick?
Remember the grief of meals in that manse?
In our walnut tree, we ate without fear,
read for hours–brothers together–

boyish infidels hiding from the blind
crusader of an angry God. You, my brother,
came down and became devout on Saturdays–
like him in your way. Part of me is still

up there–where these English leaves still
shelter me from zealotry I learned to fear.

MY AUNT, HELEN OF AVON

Sickly, small, premature,
a goatsmilk baby, hard to suckle,
she couldn't see to read. Every day
school and home were trouble.

Her mother shunned her while
her beautiful, talented sister
won scholarships to walk on water.
Her father, her only friend,

took her for long afternoons
in the Model "A" as he sold
his fireweed honey door to door
up the Depression valley.

There was only one day of joy
she could remember. At school,
Aunt Helen won a sewing contest
in the seventh grade.

Fifty years later, she still knew
her first and only prize–
touring the new dam in Alder–
the hot odor of electricity spinning.

After that, Prince Charming turned
out to be Leonard, a drunken logger she
met at church. Three sons died
childless and young. The fourth

ran as far as time would let him.
Her days came true in junk mail, clutter,
housework (she always hated), rain, TV,
wood fires, tall grass, dark rooms,

and driving her Avon route in stump
country where she could tell her best
soap, perfume, and powder customers
her story over coffee–and they loved her.

UNCLE LEONARD, PENITENT

for my cousin, Carl Falck (1948-1966)

After her son was shipped to Portland–
a grenade fragment from Vietnam–
Aunt Helen remembered Carl had said
there was no place for him to sleep
in the house when he came home–tired
from basic–in his neat fatigues.

So after cutting Weyerhauser timber
all day in his black wool underwear,
each night–taking up his pick, shovel,
and wheelbarrow–Uncle Leonard attacked
the dirt under his house to carve out
the new basement.

For a year Uncle Leonard dug, dug
faithfully, counted carefully each
shovelful he threw–55,000–
he would say–exactly 55,000
shovelfuls of dirt, and that count
gave him some incessant ache–

some countless pain beyond his back.
Eventually, the Army sent medals, ribbons,
$5,000 for his son's life. That was all most
welcome, countable, and spent quickly
for blocks, concrete, mortar, curtains,
whitewash, and carpet in the rooms.

The monument was done. You could sleep
there underground–inside this penance,
this room made of guilt, booze, and doom.
Soon, Bible class was meeting there–

taught by Leonard, the missionary's son.
Sometime, you should visit this known

soldier's tomb in Washington–the state,
that is–yes, where Rainier guards the gloom.
You can't see it from the road but I know
the way to those descending stairs and–

ELEGY FOR A MIGRATORY BEEKEEPER

(for George L. Mayo 1894-1980)

Ah, Grandfather, bring one last load of honey home.
Let it be wild clover from Moses Coulee or Palouse
a mountain range away. Let us hear you shift and slow
down the rolling summer tons, the blue homing truck,

that Chevrolet. I will call, "He's back," and run to open
the pasture gate. Let Grandma phone the Rathie girls to come
to work next week. Let me swing wide those honey house
doors again, wrestle my big brother on the sticky

floor. Ah, bring one last load of honey home, Grandfather.
We'll untie your knots, coil the hemp ropes as you yawn,
slide arthritic from the truck—beat at sixty five from
hours of crossing Snoqualmie, your bees three hundred miles

away. We'd sing "Tipperary" and "Irish Eyes" to keep awake,
remember? All night, I fed you mints, salt nuts by the sack,
Black Jack by the stick. Remember that time in Entiat?
The truckstop waitress there? We sang "Danny Boy" to her

for pie. Give us that sweet weight again, Grandfather.
We'll pry the covers off your last load and hear the hum
of that lost bee—the one who forgot to leave the comb.
She stowed away inside her cell, stung me between the eyes

to almost tears. You're that bee now, Grandfather. You're
that cell. You're buried in the valley now, and I'm still
here remembering you, Alder, that honey house, your wisdom,
art, abundance forever. Ah, give us those whitecombed fat

supers to carry in again–weight to stagger boys into men.
Fire the boiler. Let my brother Doug clean the wax melter.
Sweet steam will warm our extracting room. Blonde Alice will
wield the hot uncapping knife opening these cells to

gleam. Ah, Grandfather, bring us one last load of honey
home. As we whirl in this extracting world, let those
summers–when you taught us how to live–crystalize and come
to rest here now. My eyes are swollen shut, Grandfather,

and memory folds my hands for the strong old singer–gone.

GRANDMA WILHELMINA AT EIGHTY FIVE

I'm alone here now with cats
my windows overgrown.
I knit afghans day on day
and death waits in my room.

I've lived too long.
My Father's gone for years.
My words are slow
as moss on stone.

When my daughter comes
to check on me
I'm going to say,
"Let's get the garden in."

I've lived too many years
by this lake shore soft
above the Alder Dam–the fishing
getting worse, they say.

Nothing now I have to do.
I read and sleep and knit
grow my fingernails
more brittle, my hair green.

See my gallons of buttons
saved? My desk cluttered
with clipped obituaries
and old cards? Nothing ever

thrown away. My children live
nearby. I see my grandchildren
every day. They bring me mail,
paper, food, and company.

All my life, I believed in
Jesus, taught my little
class at Sunday School
to love the Lord.

Please tell me, tell me
one more time–
what was my maiden name
back home?

Where was I born?
How long has my Andy been gone?

THE CLOTHES OF DEAD MEN COME TO ME

by mail. Again and again. I am escaping far
away but my favorite bloodhounds of frugality
are baying after me. Somehow, I've left a track.

Here, my grandfather's last tan cotton shirts–
my grandmother sends them tied up with twine–
too many knots–in one brown paper sack.
They have all been washed, she writes, and you
are about the same size now as
he was when he died of shaking Parkinsons.
His name was George.
He fell trees and kept his bees.
Seeing these shrunk sleeves once thick with strength,
I put my nose to them, smell for honey, wax, or sting
–nothing's left but that white detergent–Tide.

Here, my cousin's cowboy shirts–pearl-button
plaid flannels. They suddenly appear from Elko
Nevada–where he drowned at 14. Riding after
cattle, his cowhorse bucked him into easy water.
He never learned to swim, went under. Every yoke
here is too small and tight for me.
His name was George.
His father–my uncle–a drunk logger, bitter,
angry over Depression poverty that
killed his hope to learn. His sons fled from him
–their lives all childless deadends. Oh uncle,
here are the empty shirts too full of grief.
I did not ask for them–too heavy to lift up.

My mother calls from California two
weeks after my stepfather's funeral, tells me she's
sending a sweater she knitted for the dead preacher.
I can't refuse her. The light cardboard box
comes from her Protestant paradise so neatly wrapped it

could be a bomb. When I see that gray cable stitch,
I recoil, throw the package from me to the floor.
It wants to insinuate itself, shrink me like some
boa constrictor, some Procrustes of blind idealism.
His name was Frank. His gospel was a steel box
with money at the center every week.

Good women of my family, please don't haunt
me more with this frugality. Please, I have had
enough of death's wardrobe to last a century.
Salvation's Army, take them—take them all—

A STORY UNCLE ERNEST TOLD

Ridges from home, he hiked the Elbe trail
through timber one Christmas night–a boy alone.
Rainier wind began to roar through giant firs
and widow makers–huge dead limbs–crashed

and broke around him–death easy on all sides.
Under a green cedar, he lit his tallow candle
in a gallon pail–crude lantern trembling light.
When the wind died back, he ran toward home.

When the storm began to blow again, he waited
under another cedar while dying deadly fir limbs
fell and fell. All night he went on like that–
between hesitate and sure–and lived to tell us all.

Can you still see him there–running green tree
to green? waiting for wind to bring old death
down, then running on again? listening and alive?
Now, tallow light trembles in your hands, in mine.

ADVICE FOR CHILDREN FROM THE COUNTRY

I.

A logger never turns his back on a log–
you'll never hear it start to roll.

Of course, all a log can do is kill you
–so don't worry about it now.

If you're going to get hurt in the woods,
do it after lunch. Why waste the whole day?

If you fall timber for wages,
let someone else sharpen your saws.

Let the crew know who's boss right away.
That will save you trouble later.

You've been on the job five minutes
and you're the boss already, huh?

To heal that smashed finger
go home and put it in cider.

II.

A hunter looks *through* the trees–
through the spaces between.

A hunter looks for parts of deer–
ears, horns, a flashing tail.
You may never see the whole.

Treat every gun as a loaded gun
until you know it's not.

Never point a gun at anything
you don't intend to shoot.

Don't shoot at anything
you don't intend to kill.

Never kill anything
you don't intend to eat.

III.

To find the best watermelon, knock.
The highest note is firm and sweet.

Water your garden in the cool—
not in the heat. Plants prefer it.

If you want aplenty to share, plant
three times what your family can eat.

"A lazy man's load" means
you're carrying too much at once.

Don't shout at a young dog.
That breaks her spirit
and she'll pee all over
when she comes in the house.

Never put your face right down
in front of a strange dog.
That means you want to fight
and you'll get bit.

IV.

Better an old queen than
no queen at all.

Give a young queen room to lay–
give her a good location–
she'll take care of the rest
all by herself.

A beekeeper makes no fast
moves around the hive.
Work the smoke gently.
Never wear dark clothes.

V.

Money is always easy to borrow
always tough to pay back.

VI.

Always leave a farmer's gate
the way you found it–
Someone probably wanted
it like that.

Don't chase the cows.
There'll be blood in the milk
pail at milking time.
That's not a pretty sight.

Don't ride the goats.
You might break their backs.

Always tie up an animal with
a bowline 'round the neck.
A slip knot will just choke
anything to death.

Never wrestle with a pig.
You'll get filthy
and the pig, well, the pig
won't know the difference.

Speak softly to the setting hen
when you gather eggs.
If you spook her, she might
abandon her nest for good.

If the rooster attacks you,
stand your ground.
If you try to run, he'll
just ruin your stockings.

If you see a ewe lying in
one place all day, she's cast.
Go out there and roll her up.
She's in a depression.

Don't turn your back on a ram.
If he thinks you're not looking,
he'll send you flying
ass over teakettle.

Before butchering, always wash
your hands carefully
and hone your knife to a feather.
Nothing should suffer.

    VII.

Right to tight, left to loose–
remember this for nuts and bolts–
except left-handed threads.
They're reverse.

Around machines, always listen
for a strange sound. If something is
going wrong, and you don't hear it
first, the damage will be done.

VIII.

A weasel in the chicken coop will
kill every hen and leave.
It just likes the taste of blood.
So always latch the door.

Never get between
a bear and her cubs.

Always leave a fawn alone.
The doe is around. You just
can't see her.

Let the trout take the bobber
under before you set the hook.

Don't go around killing things.
Everything does some good–
even if some people aren't
smart enough to see it.

OCTOBER CRABBING—OFF DESDEMONA SANDS
ASTORIA, OREGON

for Ralph Wirfs

Flying inland, the brown pelican dives out of the low
morning sky for some silver glint, some fin of the true
to keep life breathing whole and–diving–
she disappears in a sudden splash of river
water rising upward like a silver fire.
A gull shadows this headlong hurtling descent
waits for any bit of error to surface and endure.

From the gunnel, you let the crab traps sink away
into the Honeyhole. The baits are ripe
with death. We, old friends alive, fish together.
We anchor. The double crab buoys bob
across the surface–orange reminders of that
unknown life at the bottom of the world we
seek. We settle back, let the crab traps soak.
> *Here, the sea always welcomes the river*
> *the river gives itself away to the sea.*

You pour orange juice, you pour coffee.
Out of thin paper, you pull prestidigitating
cinnamon twists, triangles of sweet Danish.
Under us, a wedge of salt water has brought
Dungeness crab we cannot see scuttling
inland from the sea. They ride the tidal surge
across the floor of shifting sand to feast.

Every sandbar can be named, you say, for
the ship who died there when her men went down.
This is the threat of delta everywhere.
Those innocent white standing waves just north
killed all those Portland boys that day
and further out we know the bar is famous for great
death and grave for all craft ignorant and small.

104

Here, the sea always welcomes the river
the river gives itself away to the sea.

Even the Coast Guard pilot boats cannot
save all lives descending here. Crabs are waiting
for their feast on men who understand—too
late—where they have come, where water
has carried them. Rip tide may never let
them up for anyone to find until their bones
are beautiful with barnacles and sand.

Over coffee, the morning clouds move
inland. The bridges of Astoria seem tiny as
erector sets. We bring up years of stories—
our narrow pious fathers dying without
the slightest knowledge of their sons
other wives married to nice houses
our children lost, magnificent, jilted, loved.
> *Here, the sea always welcomes the river*
> *the river gives itself away to the sea.*

We bring up red-haired girls whose bright
lures we struck, debts to banks for half
a million bucks, murdered children, broken
houses impossible to fix that we fixed
stupid deans tossed out to save the schools
divorce, life gone crazy as a shit house mouse—
no end to wrack, to what we've seen marooned.

Pulling up the traps, sweet Dungeness
wait inside the wire. Lured by death into
being life for us, their tiny eyes bulge,
red claws beat the air. They scuttle sideways
on the deck. You teach me how to pick
them up from the back. They can hurt.
We sort and measure legals, jumbos.
> *Here, the sea always welcomes the river*
> *the river gives itself away to the sea.*

Live river crabs with barnacles and mud
fly overboard and slowly sink. A flotilla
of hungry gulls gathers, waits, stares
wants what we might accidentally kill.
There is the writhe and flail of pincers
reaching through the empty air. "We knocked
the hell out of them," you say and smile.

The catch is limits for us both–two dozen
jumbos in the bag. We count them twice–
just to be safe. The shared feast is sure, hot water
already boiling in the mind. Loaded now, *Blue Finn*
knows the way to take us in. Her lapstrake hull
cuts any wave. Her fifty steady horses hum us home.
Her bilge pump works on what we cannot see.
    Here, the sea always welcomes the river
    the river gives itself away to the sea.

Red, right, returning is the rule now. Black
broken piling mark the Hammond entrance–
one break in wet jetty rock all we need to feel.
Gleaming cormorants stare knowingly from every pile.
At the dock, I take your picture–one fat jumbo crab
writhing in each hand. Going out empty, we went
down, brought abundance up, brought it back to
speak, to share. We'll land this life until the end.
    Here, Pacific always welcomes the river
    Here, Columbia gives itself away to the sea.

THE LICHEN FAMILY STORY

Fungi and Algae loved each other
but the world was hard, bare, cold–
no flowers, people, fruit, or trees, no
dirt where roots could hide and feed.

Some eon they got married, settled
down. Together, they got the hardest job
in the world–eating rocks, making dirt.
For a 120 million years of work, Fungi

and Algae stuck together, never quit.
Their fragile quiet relatives spread out.
Can you see this pair? Their furious old
feast? Your life–a Lichen lovers' gift?

VI.

HEART OF THE VALLEY

KEYNOTE FOR MARCH 1

The silent Sunday sky rains feathers now–
sudden robins riot down the high blue afternoon
a storm maybe three hundred maybe more.
Mexico, si, maybe *Mexico* saves your life again
maybe sends them *al norte–pechicoloradas*
curving down to winter trees on slate wings of
memory and heat–nameless lives wild beyond doubt.
White rings circling their bright eyes, they perch
rest, stare, chitter incessantly, their voices calling
to each dormant bud on cold and empty limbs.

Waiting, still, alone below the university hill,
why are you so *encantado* now? Empty streets,
blank windows shining in full sun, no cars. Where
is everyone this *magnifico* deserted afternoon?
Think of those red hearts beating a thousand miles
through mapless sky to find specific earth again.
This circle coming true today started in the Pleistocene–
two million years ago and who are we? *Diga me*?
Think of their memory–*Rio Grande*, gable, hidden
crotch of tree, blue shells opening to light, round
crowded tight apartment of mud and grass, of cherries,
housecat terrorists, sweet red worms in lawns
a place to sing the long light up and down again.

Porque amo este momento ? Diga me, amor,
diga me, porque? Porque? Why do I love this
moment when robins come from *Mexico* again?
Tell me, love, tell me, why, why–in any language
that you know has wings.

DREAM IN MAY

for Barbara

Opening your window
you hear a far bell ring.
Rain all across your valley
now–a wet certain day

is ending in soft chime.
Years of sky let down
a silver streaming screen
of vast pacific sea.

Water moves all rivers
beyond capacities.
Standing naked, listening,
you stare out, wonder,

remember awe, words,
faces, hands you loved–all
return, return to you
there at the open window

where you hear the rain bell
come again again again again–
certain days ringing
beyond all names and forms.

THE HUNTER, THE DEER, THE RIVER

The hunter went into the density of brush and trees, the darkness and gold shade beside the river. He could hear the water flowing there. He laid down to wait for anything to move. He did not know exactly where he was or why he was there that day. He was a hunter, that much he knew, though he seemed to have no weapon in his hands. He knew the open spaces along the foothills and the opening spaces through the valley, but he had found nothing there to satisfy him. So he had come to the density of green brush and trees, thickets of willow and low branching alder and fir, and when he had walked as far as he could into that green world, he crawled on his hands and knees until he could crawl no more and then he rolled onto his back and began to wait for anything to move. He began to listen there in that canyon for a sound. He could not remember anyone waiting for him at home. He could not remember his name. He knew he was a hunter waiting on his back in the density of green–no weapons in his hands.

How long the hunter waited there he did not know. Time seemed to disappear. He may have slept. The sound of water may have lulled him into dream or doze. He felt safe there hidden by the density of the green world. Looking up through the crisscrossed branches, he might have seen some crosshatched blue sky. He lay quietly and waited there for anything to move.

Suddenly, beside his head, he heard a noise, a shaking. A patch of leaves and earth and branches began to move, to stand–seeming to come out of the earth right beside him. On his right, between the hunter and the river. He did not turn to see who was coming, who had awakened now, who was moving beside him. He could hear careful soft footsteps. He turned his eyes toward the sound and kept his head still. He could see four legs–tan red–standing within easy reach of his right hand. Looking higher, he saw gleaming velvet horns. With his right hand, he reached out and gripped a horn. The face of the deer turned to him, loomed directly before him. It was the most beautiful face he had ever seen–luminous brown eyes stared

112

at him but were not afraid. The ageless velvet horn filled his hand. The deer pulled against him–to be free, to lift him from his hiding place–but his weight was enough to hold them there.

They struggled against each other there–how long the hunter didn't know. Sometimes the hunter would hold onto both sides of the antlers with his hands. When he let go with his left hand, he tried to cover the deer's black nostrils with his palm, to smother the deer, but the deer just opened its mouth and breathed anew. The deer's beauty–luminous brown eyes, red heaving sides, graceful curves of thighs– became vivid, powerful, more obvious to the hunter as they struggled there. He began to doubt the wisdom of his reaching out, to doubt himself, his desire for this life that seemed to have risen out of the earth so close to him. He wondered now if the deer was part of him.

And he let go of the velvet horn and fell back into the grass and watched the deer walk silently gracefully away like a shadow through the trees. He slept then and dreamed again of entering a density of brush and trees by a river, the darkness and gold shade. He could hear the water flowing there.

NIGHT MESSENGER

A man lies in bed on his side
alone in a room far from home.
He dreams that he hears
himself calling her name–

the name of a woman he loves
who lives many mountains away.
"Help me," he hears himself call–
he doesn't know why–as though

he is awake and dreaming too.
Waiting, silent, he hears
the soft sound of a form move
behind him where he cannot see–

the rustle of a robe, bare feet
across a floor. He senses some
power approaching his spine.
He cannot turn around. From

behind, he feels her arms glide
around his chest and squeeze.
He cannot see her, yet he knows
the woman he loves has come,

the only woman whose arms
comprehend how ripeness yearns.
He recognizes her strong hands.
He feels her breasts as subtle

suns against his back. He feels
her curve her holy form
to him as though they were
matching spoons lying down

dissolving silver in some sea.
"I cannot help you there,"
she whispers in his ear.
Suddenly, the man wakes up.

JUNE NIGHT, FULL MOON

Past midnight I wake alone.
Moonlight comes–lover–to me now.
Windows wide, her luminous body

moves over my bed with soft strong
arms I sense but never feel come on.
Heaving off my sheets, I open, turn,

give all my naked dreaming life away.
She laves me with her voice, dark eyes.
Her tongue rouses me with sad cosmic

joy–a man untouched by any hands–
human or divine–two solitary years.
She illuminates me with orgasmic still

silver light, then clouds away. Alone
again, falling through the illusion of her
limbs, I cannot sleep–so full of avatar–

lips rich with the salt taste of her skin,
with how she–fearless with delight–
came over me–nightlight incarnate–

showed me the whole soul, body, mind
her sky all magnificent beyond me still.
Dreamer, oh dreamer, come again, again.

WALKING INTO THE FLOOD

Rain beat against my glass room
rain so rich I could not see, an
old summer storm so watery, vast.
Inside, waiting, I wondered where

you were. How long could I last ?
Rain intensified. Water wanted in.
My windows boomed–empty–on.
Branches in me broke and split.

Unbearable that waiting turned–
joy, fear, wondering incessantly–
I put my lover's coat on then,
went out all doors, walked into that

flood. Water falling laved my ears
silver fluted sky splashed and broke
around me everywhere, dissolved–
my life drenched with welcoming

wet sound. I filled with cries
and knew then, I was not alone.
I knew you would come to me
somehow–after that–I knew

your voice had already called me
out
of my glass self
to love.

IN THE GARDEN

after C. Austin Miles

Why come to the garden alone?
Love's dew is ripe on her roses
and the voice I hear kissing in my ear
the goddess's tongue discloses

and she laughs with me and she moves with me
and she tells me I am her love
and the joy we flare as we tremble there
none other   has ever   curved.

She comes and the cry of her voice
is so bright the stars dim their shining
and the aureole that she gives to me
within my eyes is blinding

and she laughs with me and she moves with me
and she tells me I am her love
and the joy we flare as we tremble there
none other   has ever   curved.

I lay in the garden with her
though nights around us are falling
Love bids me stay in her timeless day
her lips of fire–enlightening

and she laughs with me and she moves with me
and she tells me I am her love
and the joy we flare as we tremble there
none other   has ever   curved.

A RITUAL FOR RECEIVING THE GIFT
OF A BOWL OF FRUIT

Oh, red grapes round in light. Taste two
first– clusters oh so holy ripe invite your
tongue to savor their cool burning skin.

Deeper, orange sections gleam–a bed of
juicy wordless trinities abide. Take one in
your teeth–oh sacrament–peel, suck in.

Underneath, red melon pieces swim–
oh succulent jumble, oh sacred flowering.
Dive, let your lips find one, come up, breathe–

if you can–before red grapes call your
name out of the whispering bowl of sky
saying taste and see again, again, again.

JULY MORNING SONG AT 5:30 A.M.

A black cow grazes the green mountain
her steep-sided pasture browning out in heat.

One mottled pigeon teeters on that parapet–
square brick where no angelus will ring.

One red squirrel dances on this cable
sends highwire taunts to the dogs below–

body of her father flattened in the street.
One tree swallow rows her blue-green wings

above the silent trees, fishing for her children
mosquitoes too scarce for words and behind

her comes the Vaux swift beating faster oars,
her soft gray soaring hunger through the air.

Believing houses sleep. They trust electric gods
will not suddenly surge, ignite their dreams of ease.

Empty streets stare around the corner curbs
fire hydrants wonder if their secret lives will be

opening today. At the jail, the middle-aged mason
named Rick climbs his high steel scaffolding

steps on a narrow plank, balances his weight,
bangs his pointed trowel on his wheel barrow

starts mixing the first batch of mortar, another

day of concrete blocks. His face is sunburned, sore.

From a high window, two naked feet start out–
ten pink toes wiggle in the early summer light.

They belong to you who–one July day–woke up
saw pattern beyond belief–so so precarious our

common life, all so balanced on the edge of death.

A DREAM OF TWO

In her dark kitchen,
a woman sits at peace on her floor
looking at a man she loves. He
sits before her there. They are naked now
but do not touch. They do not speak.
Each is empty of all fear, all desire.
They seem to be trees living by some
underground river quietly flowing
out of each
other.

In the space between them,
a heap of bright leaves gleams
as though soft diamond light flowed
like huge water up from underground.
They do not know where those burning
leaves have come from or where they go
or how that light came to flow mysterious
unconsumed
between them
there.

In their shared stillness,
the woman studies his shadow, seems
to add another leaf, then the man does
the same. Nothing they can do
seems to change
the light from the leaves
the shadows playing over
them. There is so much

they cannot
understand

so much peace between
them there–they do not want
to, cannot
move.

ALL EMPTINESS IS FULL

Tonight, love, your bowl is all
I have to hold, the cool curving form
so open, tapered, balanced, round–
an emptied vessel in my hands. Still,

inside the lip, fecundity weaves on–
grapes, pears, strawberries, leaves.
Here, sweet and ancient images of
female earth are fired in clay relief

and raised by design–just enough–for
my braille fingertips to feel. Still,
I see you entering my room, holding
this full bowl in your right hand.

"Apple salad," you said, smiling,
your voice so ripe and succulent
I could not breathe, your memory
now more cornucopia than any

body can contain. Still, late, alone,
I taste your lips of dream, wonder
where you sleep. This empty bowl
overflows. The feast goes on.

HIGH CASCADES

love pacific rain, curve
wind, bear old storms, explode,
turn ice to glacier lily bloom.
Hear that first tick of melting

snow? Meadow blue with awe?
Hear springs seep, creeks clatter,
white water roar, falls pour
wet thunder, mist, rainbow

spray? Oh range so fragile, dangerous
your beauty washes every face
your flow redeems the stone. Thirsty
for the true, we take you in.

WATER MUSIC, THE UPPER IMNAHA RIVER

For Barbara

The old voice of the rain turned our
clear creeks into one silver river that
afternoon. We wandered upstream together
–hand in hand through the Twin Lakes burn–
that forest of black dead standing trees
listening to our slow footsteps fall.

Sun came along. We studied white snags,
with black branches, black snags with
white branches, stopped, kissed, went
slowly on, stopped, kissed again.
Over fallen needles of the trail, we saw
pine trunks torn by bears for food, firs

carved with cavities for new homes.
You named *rudbeckia*, larkspur–lives
so close and new I could not tell them
from my own. You named the downy tapping,
seeking sustenance on the burned lodgepole.
Where a clear creek chattered on beside

a purple giant boulder and black snag,
I put red ripe thimbleberry on your tongue.
You found a small orange moth, showed
me wings, laid them in the dust again.
Under those black dead standing trees,
fireweed multiplied its graceful redpink

phoenix plumes. Wildfire–destroyer, creator–
made this beauty germinate, flower, fill
with nectar now. Wild bees hummed

through that understory of sweet bloom.
We understood. We too have been through terror
burned, fought, refused to die, regenerated with

roots in memory too fine for words.
Crossing the wilderness boundary,
one sudden hummingbird streaked up
perched its green iridescent wings, one
chambered beating heart in the center
of that forest of dead trees. We heard

the river flowing over stones. You said
the light on riffles was the same as light
that gleamed on the black cracked snags
stripped dead and clean–cubed columns
of charcoal spires sixty feet in the air.
We marveled there, held our easy way

together all that afternoon, joined by
that world we found–alive, magnificent,
old fire flowering among dead trees.
All that old burnt heartwood, we knew,
must fall finally down to feed the wild
lives who come to flourish now.

We were strong enough that day to
listen without divisions, our separate
selves moving together the way tanagers
fly. Eating apples at the Blue Hole,
we saw love's silver water gather, flow,
blend, swirl, cut through stone forever.

ACKNOWLEDGMENTS

I want to thank these editors and publishers—listed here alphabetically by title of publication—for first publishing and/or reprinting the poems included in this collection. Titles revised in this collection are in ( ). Also, my thanks to Eastern Oregon University which granted me a summer stipend that allowed me to finish this book; to those anonymous Oregon literati who supported the publication of this collection; to those writers, poets, and critics who gave insightful pre-publication blurbs. David Memmott—publisher, poet, fiction writer, reviewer, arts advocate—must be recognized here for his faithful, passionate, and professional commitment to literary life in general and to this book in particular.

ARTE (National Council of Teachers of English). Urbana, IL, Jack Lorts, editor, for reprinting my part of "Great Oregon Serial Poem." Vol. 5 No. 3, 1995: 5. (Poetry, That Bandit)

Clearwater Journal, La Grande, OR, Sandy Gullickson and John Daniel, editors, for "Fence Post Talks." Vol. 1, No. 1, 1982: 47. (Professors–In Their Masks...)

Columbia River Intertribal Fish Commission News, Portland, OR, Elizabeth Smith, editor, for "Dialogue At Buckhorn Lookout." Vol. 8, No. 2, 1985: 7.

Creative Voices: An Eastern Voice Supplement, La Grande, OR, Cherie Murray, editor, for "Passing the Violinist's House." Nov. 9, 1994: 4.

Gleanings in Bee Culture, Medina, OH, Mark Bruner, editor, for "Invoking a Migratory Beekeeper." Vol. 111, No. 9, Sept. 1983: 497. (Elegy for a Migratory Beekeeper.)

Hubbub, Portland, OR, Lisa Steinman and Jim Shugrue, editors, for "Segues for Interstate 84." September, 1998, 33-37.

Jefferson Monthly, Ashland, OR, Vince and Patty Wixon, editors, for "Excuses in Snow." Vol. 22, No 12. December, 1998, 35. "A Wilderness Man in the Great City." October, 1995: 35.

KSOR Guide to the Arts, Ashland, OR, Vince and Patty Wixon, editors, for "A Father Speaks to His Son...." Feb. 1986: 40. "Trying Out." Feb 1986: 42. "January: A Letter." Feb. 1986: 43.

Northwest Writers, Inc, Portland, OR, Karen Swenson, judge, for "The Emperor Breeds Only on the Ice," Andres Berger Poetry Prize, 1994

Oregon East, La Grande, OR, Randy Kromwall, editor, for "Point Guard Bringing the Ball Up Court." XXVII, 1996: 23.

Oregon East, La Grande, OR, John Pankl, editor, for "Coyote Creates Yellowjacket From the Bones of Job." Vol. XXIII, 1992: 73-4.

Oregon English, Portland, OR, Ulrich Hardt, editor, for "The Emperor Breeds Only On The Ice." Vol. XI, 1989; "Great Oregon Serial Poem." Vol. XIII, No. 2, Fall, 1991:16-19. (Poetry, That Bandit). "Star." XIX No. 1, Spring, 1997: 17.

Oregon Zoo, Portland, OR, John Fraser, et al, judges, for "High Cascades" and "The Lichen Family Story," works permanently installed in Cascade Crest Exhibition, 1998.

Poetry Northwest, Seattle, WA, David Wagoner, editor, for "Safeway Conversation." Vol. 22, No. 2 1981: 20. "Five Six Minutes in March." Vol. 22, No. 2 1981: 19. "The Trail to School." Vol. 21, No. 1 1980: 53 (The Black Wolf of Love) "Fable." Vol. 21, No. 1 1980: 54. (Fable for An Arrogant Century)

Portland Lights: A Poetry Anthology. Steven Nemirow and Barbara LaMorticella, eds. for "On Burnside." Portland: OR, Press 22, 1999: 17.

*Stafford's Road: An Anthology of Poems for William Stafford.*Adrienne Lee Press, Monmouth, OR, 1991. Tom Ferte, editor, for "The Cagy Laureate of Oregon." 36-7.

Talking River Review, Lewiston, ID, Paul Tinsley, editor, for "A.J. Dickey Couldn't Run the Ends." Winter, 1998, 117

The Kerf, Crescent City, CA, Anita Cumbra, Ken Letko, et al, editors, for "Excuses in Snow." May, 1998, 22-23

Author Photo by Jan Boles (1994)

In 1995, after he won the Andres Berger Award in Poetry from Northwest Writers, Inc., *The Oregonian* described George Venn (1943—) as one of "the best-known and most respected poets in the state." His poems have appeared in uncommon places: the Ron Finne film, *Tamanawis Illahee*; a Native American tribal newsletter, a wilderness dedication, a national beekeeping journal, National Public Radio guides, Portland's New Oregon Zoo, lyrics set to music by American composers—Eversole, Tomasetti, McKinnon—and performed by touring choirs and soloists. Born in the shadow of the Washington Cascades, Venn's early life was divided between his parents' city manses and churches and his grandparents' country farmhouse, woods, and apiary, between the Alder, Washington, of his childhood and Spirit Lake, Idaho, the burned-over milltown of his adolescence, between cedars in rain and tamarack gone gold, death of his father and his mother's remarriage. In 1967—after studying in Equador, Spain, and England—he graduated from the College of Idaho. In 1970, he completed an MFA at the University of Montana and was appointed to the faculty at Eastern Oregon University. His early poems were published by Prescott Street Press— **Sunday Afternoon: Grande Ronde** and **Off the Main Road**— and in 1987, Oregon State University Press published **Marking the Magic Circle**, a complex multi-genre collage. From 1989-94, Venn served as General Editor for the 2,000 page historical anthology, **THE OREGON LITERATURE SERIES**. (Awards on back cover.) Currently, he is Writer-in-Residence at Eastern Oregon University, La Grande.

ICE RIVER PRESS is an imprint of Wordcraft of Oregon established to publish Eastern Oregon writers of fiction and poetry whose work falls outside the literary fabulist/speculative tradition which is the primary focus of Wordcraft Speculative Writers Series. Ice River Press books feature writers with a strong sense of the region, its history, its voices, its aspirations. Most Ice River Press titles will be saddle-stitched chapbooks (up to 40 pages) with occasional publication of full-length books.

This book was designed using Wordperfect 8 on a Pentium system and output on a Hewlitt Packard 2100 Series PCL6. The cover photo is of the Grande Ronde River by David Jensen, and the cover design is by Brian C. Clarke. The book was printed as a limited edition of 1,000 trade paperback copies in the United States by Complete Reproduction Service, Inc., of Santa Ana, CA.

Other Books by Ice River Press

The Kingdom at Hand, a chapbook-length poem by David Axelrod, winner of the 1992 Carolyn Kizer Prize for Poetry. ISBN: 1-877655-09-0, 1993, 40 pgs., $5, signed & numbered.

Graves in Wheat, poems by Thomas Madden, ISBN: 1-877655-22-8, 1998, 56 pgs. , perfectbound, $7.95

Distributors for Wordcraft of Oregon books are Small Press Distribution and Bookpeople. Books may be ordered through bookstores or on-line through Amazon.com.